A CHRISTIAN JOURNEY

Religious poems from life's experiences

by Thomas E. Williams

Copyright 2012 by Thomas E. Williams

All rights reserved.

For information contact Tom Williams at

achristianjourney777@gmail.com.

Dedication

To my daughter, Michaila, and my sons, Justin, Ryan, and Rick. They are the joys of my life and true gifts from God.

To my parents, Ed and Shirley Williams, who taught me virtues, morals, and set many good examples for me by the way they lived. They encouraged me to regularly attend church although they rarely did themselves. And, as they grew older, they seemed to forget all the trouble I was as a child. (Thank God for a parent's biased love.)

To Frank and Mildred Vess, great neighbors who faithfully took me to church every Sunday that I wanted to go from the time I was seven years old until I could drive myself.

To Henry Wills, who on many occasions fasted and prayed on my behalf that I might find salvation before I finally did.

To Rev. Steve Fletcher and Rev. Norman Moore, who during the early days of their ministries were youth pastors who helped to guide me in the proper direction.

And, to Martin Gjonovich, Dorothea Brown, Jack and Lois Williams, Rev. Leo Johnston, missionary Marie Lind, Josie Villalobos, Kathy Butler, and Paul Hink for their exemplary Christian lives that influenced my life.

Contents

Introduction 1

O Lord My God 3

When I Accept Jesus 6

He Died For You and For Me 9

Have Faith in God 12

I Have Found Him 14

Let Jesus Christ Come In...17

The Lord Is Walking With Me..................................19

I'm On the Right Road Now....................................22

Leave Your Burdens All to Me 25

How Can I Be a Loser...27

I'm Going Home 29

I Know of a Man 31

Walking Life's Road 33

Lead Me Home..35

The Sea of Life...37

I Can't Help But Rejoice..40

We Advertise Our Name 43

They Called Him Savior 46

Without Love I'd Be Nothing 48

Betrayed, Denied, Forsaken 51

A Change Come Over Me 54

He Rolled the Stone Away.. 56

There's A Great Day Coming 59

Molded Man 62

One of These Days 65

Let the Blessings Flow 67

It's Just Me and Jesus 70

My Prayer 73

You Can't Buy Your Way Into Heaven 75

Solutions From You 78

He's Standing at Your Heart 80

I Have Heaven to Live For 82

Who Do You Say I Am 84

I Would Have Never Made It On My Own 87

Introduction

Each Christian journey is unique and a very personal one. Some seem to have clear skies and straight paths with few if any obstacles, while others may experience stormy weather and find many roadblocks and detours along the way. There are also those who choose to turn and go their own way possibly never to return.

Mine has not been a smooth one, but throughout my journey, whether on the right path or while having strayed, God has been there watching over me. There have been many lessons for me to learn and probably more to come. The rough places along the way have made me a better person, increased my faith, and have made the "smooth rides" even more appreciated and enjoyable.

1 Corinthians 10:13 (GNT) tells us, *"Every test that you have experienced is the kind that normally comes to people. But God keeps his promise, and he will not allow you to be tested beyond your power to remain firm; at the time you are put to the test, he will give you the strength to endure it, and so provide you with a way out."* I've found that so true.

Throughout my teen and young adult years I wrote a number of songs about my search for God, my relationship with Him, and other things related to my Christian journey. I was fortunate to have had the opportunity to sing at many churches and share these songs during those years. For the past few decades though, the songs have been little more than lyric sheets in a binder sitting on a closet shelf. Those song lyrics are presented here, in chronological order as written, as a book of poems with the hope that the reader will find at least one of them to be inspiring, comforting, or in some other manner helpful in their search for, or journey with, our Lord.

"The Lord bless you and keep you; the Lord make his face shine on you and be gracious to you; the Lord turn his face toward you and give you peace." – Numbers 6:24-26 (NIV)

"Hear my cry, O God; attend unto my prayer."
— Psalms 61:1 (KJV)

O Lord My God
(Prayer of a Sinner)

O Lord my God,

I want to be a Christian.

To live my life

The way it ought to be.

But, God you know

I'm nothing but a sinner.

Take hold my hand,

O Lord, guide me.

O Lord my God,

Listen to this sinner.

Lord, listen to

This sinner's plea.

Almighty God,

I need you more than ever.

I pray, dear God,

Deliver me...

From temptations of the devil.

From all forms of evil.

Lord, give me strength, I pray,

To be a witness to others,

A kind and loving brother.

O Lord, let me live the Christian way.

And, Lord my God,

When my time has ended,

When I pass on

To eternity,

Lord, let me go,

Let me go to Heaven

To live a life

Eternally with Thee.

"Come to Me, all who are weary and heavy-laden, and I will give you rest." - Matthew 11:28 (NASB)

When I Accept Jesus

I know someday,

I know some way,

I'll touch the hand of God.

Then I'll know

That peace and joy

That Christians talk about.

I will walk and talk with God.

I will feel His precious love.

That day when I accept Jesus as my Lord.

I know that Satan

Will do his best

To make me turn away,

But that will give me

All the more reason

To live for God every day.

He'll be my strength and my guide.

I know He'll never leave my side

After I accept Jesus as my Lord.

I'm lost in a world of sin.

I need God's hand to guide me.

And, someday I'm going to let him in

To save and sanctify me.

Listen sinner,

Does your heart cry out

For something that it lacks?

Call on Jesus,

He'll forgive you

Of every sin in your past.

He'll cleanse your heart and make it whole,

Give new life to your soul,

That day when you

Accept Jesus as your Lord.

Just trust in Jesus and He will save your soul.

"For God so loved the world, that he gave his only begotten Son, that whosoever believeth in him should not perish, but have everlasting life. For God sent not his Son into the world to condemn the world; but that the world through him might be saved." – John 3:16-17 (KJV)

He Died For You and For Me

Two thousand years ago

At a place called Golgotha's Hill,

On a cross between two thieves

Christ died to save the world.

He gave His life,

His everything

There at Calvary.

He gave His life

That we might live.

He died for you and for me.

A crown of thorns was placed on His head.

The people laughed and jeered.

The crowd held not one sorry soul.

The crowd shed not one tear.

He gave His life,

His everything

There at Calvary.

He gave His life

That we might live.

He died for you and for me.

Darkness hovered o'er the land.

The sun refused to shine.

The earth then gave a violent quake.

God's will had been done.

He gave His life,

His everything

There at Calvary.

He gave His life

That we might live.

He died for you and for me.

"And Jesus answering saith unto them, 'Have faith in God.'"
- Mark 11:22 (KJV)

Have Faith in God

In time of sorrow, in time of tears,

Cry not, brother, your Lord is near.

By your side He'll always stay

Through the darkest night

Or the stormiest day.

In time of trials, in time of fear,

Just keep in mind your in God's care.

His hand of love is guiding you.

So, have faith in God.

He'll help you through.

Faith in God can move the highest mountain.

Faith in God can calm the raging sea.

Faith in God can solve your biggest problems.

Put your faith in God and you will see.

When you are troubled or feeling low,

When you need help, pray to the Lord.

He understands because He cares.

So, have faith in God.

He answers prayer.

Faith in God can move the highest mountain.

Faith in God can calm the raging sea.

Faith in God can solve your biggest problems.

Put your faith in God and you will see.

"These things I have spoken to you, that My joy may remain in you, and that your joy may be full." – John 15:11 (NKJV)

I Have Found Him

Oh, I have found Him.

I've found a wonderful friend

In Jesus,

Christ Jesus,

Savior of man.

Oh, what a feeling.

A feeling as never before

Now that Jesus,

Christ Jesus,

Has control.

And oh, oh, what joy,

What joy now fills my soul

Since Jesus,

Christ Jesus,

Made me whole.

Now I'm no longer alone.

I've got Jesus as my guide.

And no matter how dark the night

He stays close by my side.

Oh, what a Savior.

What peace and love He will bring

If you'll open

Your heart to Jesus

And let Him in.

Just open

Your heart to Jesus

And let him in.

"Grace and peace be multiplied unto you through the knowledge of God, and of Jesus our Lord" – 2 Peter 1:2 (KJV)

Let Jesus Christ Come In

Does your life have something missing?

Do you long for peace within?

Does your past look dark and gloomy

And your future gray and dim?

When small problems become burdens

And your troubles seem to grow,

Get down on your knees and pray to Christ.

Ask the Lord to take control.

Let the Lord take over everything.

Put your faith and trust in Him.

Soon you'll find your burdens easing up.

You'll have peace of mind again.

When the road of life gets hard to walk

And trials have brought you down.

When frustrations seem an overload

And the world is closing 'round,

If you feel your life's a wasteful thing

And it's time you made a change,

Ask the Lord to come and take control.

Let Jesus be your King.

Let the Lord take over everything.

Put your faith and trust in Him.

Soon you'll find your burdens easing up.

You'll have peace of mind again.

And, your life is more enjoyable.

You are satisfied within.

All because one day you opened up

And let Jesus Christ come in.

"...and, lo, I am with you always, even unto the end of the world." – Matthew 28:20b (KJV)

The Lord Is Walking With Me

The Lord is walking with me.

I need never fear.

For He is watching o'er me;

My Jesus' always near.

He strengthens me in sorrows.

He turns me from the wrong.

And, when life's pathway darkens,

He leads me safely home.

The Lord is always with me.

He stays right by my side.

When I need someone to talk to,

In Him I can confide.

To Him I tell my troubles,

My burdens, and my needs.

I put my faith in Jesus.

He sets my mind at ease.

How happy since I've found Him.

How lovely life now is.

For now I have found Jesus.

I'm glad to be called his.

The Lord will never leave me.

Of that I can be sure.

Forever He'll be with me,

My Strength and Comforter.

And, when the time comes for me

To pass to my reward,

I'll still be with my Jesus

There in my heavenly home.

"In the way of righteousness is life, and in its pathway there is no death" – Proverbs 12:28 (NKJV)

I'm On the Right Road Now

I'm on the right road now.

I'm on the right road now.

I look ahead and see my Savior there.

I know I'm on the right road now.

For many years I wandered

In a world of sin.

I didn't know the proper way

To let the Savior in.

I walked into a church one day.

I heard the preacher speak.

He said, "Come to the altar, son,

Your Savior you will meet."

I'm on the right road now.

I'm on the right road now.

I look ahead and see my Savior there.

I know I'm on the right road now.

He all my sins has washed away.

He has cleansed my soul.

My heart is now a snowy white

Instead of black as coal.

Now every day's a bright, bright day

With Jesus there in sight.

And, in my heart there is this song

For Jesus now is mine.

I'm on the right road now.

I'm on the right road now.

I look ahead and see my Savior there.

I know I'm on the right road now.

"Cast your burden on the Lord, and He shall sustain you; He shall never permit the righteous to be moved."
- Psalm 55:22(NKJV)

Leave Your Burdens All to Me

There are times when I feel lonely.

There are times when I feel blue.

But, the Lord is watching o'er me

And He knows my problems, too.

And, no matter what the trouble

Nor whatever my burden may be,

He says, "Lay them at my feet, son.

Leave your burdens all to me.

Leave your burdens all to me."

Many times my load grows heavy,

But the Lord can make it light.

I just take it all to Jesus

For He will might it right.

And, when the sea of life gets stormy,

For me to fear there is no need.

He says, "Lay them at my feet, son.

Leave your burdens all to me.

Leave your burdens all to me."

He says, "Lay them at my feet, son.

Leave your burdens all to me."

"What shall we then say to these things? If God be for us, who can be against us? He that spared not his own Son, but delivered him up for us all, how shall he not with him also freely give us all things?" - Romans 8:31-32 (KJV)

How Can I Be a Loser

I've known folks who say they're born losers,

That their only luck has been bad.

They live in a world of self-pity.

They spend their time feeling sad.

There was a time I too walked among them

Until Christ changed my heart and my mind.

Now, how can I be a loser

When I've got the Lord on my side?

Tell me, how can I be a loser

When the Lord is walking with me?

He gives me strength and courage.

He supplies my every need.

Give my friends the world if they want it,

But give me the love of my God.

For how can I be a loser

When I've got the Lord on my side?

"In my Father's house are many mansions: if it were not so, I would have told you. I go to prepare a place for you. And if I go and prepare a place for you, I will come again, and receive you unto myself; that where I am, there ye may be also." – John 14:2-3 (KJV)

I'm Going Home

Well, praise the Lord!

I'm going home.

For many years I've walked the straight and narrow

Fighting off the devil left and right.

But, someday soon my trials will be over.

I'm going up to Heaven bye and bye.

And, praise the Lord!

I'm going home.

Going home just beyond the river.

Going home to Heaven's golden shore.

Going home – I'm going to meet my Savior.

Going home to praise Him evermore.

Someday Christ will come to get His children.

Somewhere in that number I will be.

He's coming soon to take us all to Heaven.

A mansion's up there waiting just for me.

And, praise the Lord!

I'm going home.

Going home just beyond the river.

Going home to Heaven's golden shore.

Going home – I'm going to meet my Savior.

Going home to praise Him evermore.

"Gossip is spread by wicked people; they stir up trouble and break up friendships." - Proverbs 16:28 (GNT)

I Know of a Man

I know of a man who once was a Christian.

A man who at one time lived for God.

But, one day something happened

That scarred his reputation.

A story I'm about to tell you of.

This man once took an interest

In a certain young woman.

A woman he believed was quite refined.

But, the woman's reputation was not that of a lady.

And, the people's talk about them was unkind.

The things they did together you would not call disgraceful,

But the people's gossip made them sound that way.

This gossip came from church folk

He worshipped with on Sunday.

And, from the Lord these people made him stray.

Yes, one day something happened

That scarred his reputation.

It was nothing until gossip did its job.

Gossip turned a molehill into a mighty mountain.

A mountain between this man and God.

"You will show me the path of life; in Your presence is fullness of joy..." – Psalms 16:11 (NKJV)

Walking Life's Road

Well, here I am walking down the road of life all alone.

Got a load of burdens I'm trying to carry on my own.

Don't know just what I should do.

Got no friends that I can turn to.

So, I guess I'll walk on all alone.

Down the road I met a man who asked, "Brother, have you got some time?"

I'd like to tell you about Christ Jesus, He's my Savior and a friend of mine.

I see you've got some burdens to bear.

Just tell them to Jesus, He's a friend who cares.

And, as you walk life's road, He'll ease your load.

So, now I walk that road of life, but no longer am alone.

I've got a friend who walks with me and He helps to carry my load.

Now I've peace within my soul

For Jesus has washed and made me whole.

And, He has promised me a heavenly home at the end of life's road.

Yes, at the end of life's road I've got a heavenly home!

"Teach me your way, Lord; lead me in a straight path..."
— Psalms 27:11 (NIV)

Lead Me Home

Lord, I've turned from the things that you had taught me.

I have strayed from that straight and narrow road.

I have turned my back on friends and on my family.

Now I ask, oh Lord, please lead me home.

Lord, I turned away from what I once had believed in.

I forgot that you're the Way, the Truth, and the Life.

Now I ask that you have mercy and forgive me.

And, lead me home to live the life I know is right.

Lead me home to the place where I belong, Lord.

Take me back to the life that I once knew.

Lead me home; release me from this world that holds me.

Give me back that life I had walking with you.

Lord, I left your side and planned to go on without you.

I had thought that I could make it on my own.

But, I found without my God, I am nothing.

Now I ask forgiveness Lord; please lead me home.

Lead me home to the place where I belong, Lord.

Take me back to the life that I once knew.

Lead me home; release me from this world that holds me.

Give me back that life I had walking with you.

"And there ariseth a great storm of wind, and the waves beat into the boat, insomuch that the boat was now filling. And He...rebuked the wind, and said unto the sea, 'Peace, be still.' And the wind ceased, and there was a great calm. And He said unto them, 'Why are ye fearful? Have ye not yet faith?'" – Mark 4:37-40 (ASV)

The Sea of Life

For years my earthly father

Was a sea-going man.

He captained many ships

And sailed the seas to many lands.

He traveled in calm weather

And over troubled seas,

And when that harbor came in sight,

He must have felt a certain peace.

Lord, just as my father,

I have a sea to sail.

That sea is the sea of life

And I must sail it well.

For if I should sink, Lord,

Then where would I be?

But, if I make the harbor, Lord,

There Heaven waits for me.

Sailing that sea of life

To Heaven's golden shore.

Once I make that harbor,

My journey will be o'er.

For there a home awaits me

For all eternity.

Yes, I'll make Heaven's harbor, Lord,

By staying close to Thee.

So please take the helm, Lord,

And guide me safely through.

When the seas 'round me are raging,

I'll put my faith in you.

For with your hand to guide me

I know all will be well.

I'll reach the harbor safely,

Life's sea no more to sail.

"Rejoice in the Lord always. Again I will say, rejoice!"
- Philippians 4:4 (NKJV)

I Can't Help But Rejoice

I can't help but rejoice,

Lift up my voice,

And say, "Praise God!"

For all He has given

And all the great things he has done.

He has taken my life,

Turned the darkness to light,

And shown me a path to walk on.

He has promised to keep me

And never forsake me

Regardless of what may come.

I can't help but rejoice,

Lift up my voice,

And say, "Praise God!"

For all He has given

And all the great things he has done.

Though a sinner was I,

He sent down to die

His only begotten Son.

So that when the time comes

For me to pass on,

I will have an eternal home.

I can't help but rejoice,

Lift up my voice,

And say, "Praise God!"

For all He has given

And all the great things he has done.

When at judgment I stand

He'll take hold of my hand

And say, "My child, well done!"

Through temptations and trials

It was well worth it all

For life with Jesus has only begun.

"Watch your life and doctrine closely. Persevere in them, because if you do, you will save both yourself and your hearers." - 1 Timothy 4:16 (NIV)

We Advertise Our Name

So much today is bought and sold

According to its name.

The way they advertise these days

Is somewhat like a game.

They advertise in such a way

To make us think they're best.

They plant their name into our minds

So we'll forget the rest.

And, even we in daily life

Advertise our name.

There are people watching us to see

If we live as we claim.

And, if we claim to know the Lord

And follow after Him,

We'd best be sure we advertise

The love He gives within.

For as Christians we are called

To live a certain way.

We advertise the name of Christ

In all we do and say.

And, if we want for others

To come to know His name,

We need to know the life He lived

And live ours just the same.

So, in all you do and all you say

Glorify His name.

When others notice what you have,

They should want the same.

And, once they open up their heart

And let Christ be their guest,

They'll realize what you advertise

Truly is the best.

"For there is born to you this day in the city of David a Savior, who is Christ the Lord." – Luke 2:11 (NKJV)

They Called Him Savior

He was born some time ago in the town of Bethlehem.

For thirty years He lived His life as just a common man.

But, the three years that then followed, He preached throughout the land.

He proved himself as Son of God and Savior of man.

He healed the sick, gave sight to blind, and even raised the dead.

"He who believes in me will have eternal life," He said.

With miracles that He performed and parables He told,

He taught the power and love of God to young and to old.

And, they called Him, "Savior"; they called Him, "Lord."

The heavenly Messiah of whom the scriptures had foretold.

And, every place to which He went, great crowds would come to see.

They found that He was everything that He had claimed to be.

The Jewish leaders of that day despised and hated Him.

They said that He had blasphemed God; that He was just a man.

They arrested Him for claiming that He was the Son of God.

They convicted Him and sentenced Him to die upon the cross.

But, it proved Him Savior, it proved Him Lord,

When three days after He had died, Christ arose!

And, then He told his followers, "You believe for you've seen me,

But blessed more is he who has not seen and yet believes."

"And now abide faith, hope, love, these three; but the greatest of these is love." - 1 Corinthians 13:13 (NKJV)

Without Love I'd Be Nothing

I could have faith so strong

It could move a mountain,

Hope so real

It could part the sea,

But if I had no love within my heart,

I'd be nothing.

I could have the gift

Of prophesy,

Understand

Each mystery,

But if I had no love

Within my heart,

I'd be nothing.

Love is kind.

It suffers long.

Love is forgiving.

It forgets the wrong.

Love never fails.

It is always true.

Love is what Christ has

For you.

Jesus gave His life

For me and for you.

Now He offers

His love to us, too.

And, if I didn't have

His love in my heart,

I'd be nothing.

If I didn't have

Christ's love in my heart,

I'd be nothing.

"Pilate said to them, 'What then shall I do with Jesus who is called Christ?' They all said to him, 'Let Him be crucified!' Then the governor said, 'Why, what evil has He done?' But they cried out all the more, saying, 'Let Him be crucified!'"
- Matthew 27:22-23 (NKJV)

Betrayed, Denied, Forsaken

Betrayed, denied, forsaken.

How my Lord must have felt that day

As He walked that road to Mount Calvary.

There to die, all our sins to pay.

He had been betrayed by Judas

With a kiss that meant His death.

It was a signal to the soldiers

To show them the one to arrest.

As the high priest questioned Jesus,

Nearby Peter stood looking on.

Someone said, "You're one of his disciples."

But, he denied having known Christ at all.

Then as Jesus stood at His trial,

No one spoke up in His defense.

Betrayed, then denied, now forsaken,

They sentenced Him to death.

He had come to bring salvation

And eternal life in Heaven above.

But, they chose to crucify Him.

They chose to shun the Savior's love.

Then He walked to Calvary's mountain

Burdened with the load of all sin.

Though betrayed, denied, and forsaken was He,

Still He died so that we might live.

"Therefore, if anyone is in Christ, he is a new creation; old things have passed away; behold, all things have become new." - 2 Corinthians 5:17 (NKJV)

A Change Come Over Me

I wake up in the morning with a smile upon my face

And a joy in my heart for a change has taken place.

I've a peace in my soul that there never used to be.

For since I met Jesus, there's been a change come over me.

I don't go to places where I used to sometimes go.

I don't run around with the friends I used to know.

I'm living a new life quite unlike it used to be.

For since I met Jesus, there's been a change come over me.

There's been a change come over me.

Yes, a change come over me.

I'm living a new life.

Now from sin I've been set free.

I'm walking a new pathway He lights before my feet.

Since I met Jesus, there's been a change come over me.

I wake up in the morning with a smile upon my face

And a joy in my heart for a change has taken place.

I've a peace in my soul that there never used to be.

For since I met Jesus, there's been a change come over me.

"Then Jesus...came to the tomb. It was a cave, and a stone lay against it. Jesus said, 'Take away the stone.' ...He cried with a loud voice, 'Lazarus, come forth!' And he who had died came out..." – John 11:38-44 (NKJV)

He Rolled the Stone Away

Lazarus was Jesus' dear friend.

Jesus heard that Lazarus was dead.

At the tomb where Lazarus lay,

He said, "Roll the stone away!"

And, out walked Lazarus, redeemed from the dead.

He rolled the stone away

And gave new life that day.

The one who had been dead now was living.

He rolled the stone away

And gave new life that day.

Through Jesus' saving grace a new life was given.

I was dead in a world of sin.

My lifestyle had trapped me therein.

Then Jesus came along

And He rolled away the stone.

And then, for me, a new life began.

He rolled the stone away

And gave new life that day.

The one who had been dead now was living.

He rolled the stone away

And gave new life that day.

Through Jesus' saving grace a new life was given.

My friend, how is it with you?

Will your sins be the death of you?

Ask forgiveness of those sins

And let Jesus dwell within,

And then, my friend, you will say, too…

He rolled the stone away

And gave new life that day.

The one who had been dead now was living.

He rolled the stone away

And gave new life that day.

Through Jesus' saving grace a new life was given.

"Let not your heart be troubled: ye believe in God, believe also in me. In my Father's house are many mansions: if it were not so, I would have told you. I go to prepare a place for you. And if I go and prepare a place for you, I will come again, and receive you unto myself; that where I am, there ye may be also." - John 14:1-3 (KJV)

There's A Great Day Coming

There's a great day coming

When to Heaven I'll be going.

How I'm looking forward to that coming day.

All my friends who've gone before me

I will see again in Glory

When the Lord comes to take me home with Him someday.

That man who prayed and fasted

For me when lost in darkness,

I'll see him again when I get there.

And, just to see my Jesus

For this I am most anxious.

What a glorious reunion we will have up there.

I'll walk the streets of gold there.

Sing praises to my Savior.

I'll live in a mansion Jesus made just to be mine.

Yes, there's a great day coming

When to Heaven I'll be going.

And, Lord you can come and take me home anytime.

My brother, are you ready?

Are you prepared and waiting?

The Lord is coming back and coming soon.

Forsake those worldly pleasures.

Prepare for Heaven's treasures.

For when He returns, He wants to come for you.

I'll walk the streets of gold there.

Sing praises to my Savior.

I'll live in a mansion Jesus made just to be mine.

Yes, there's a great day coming

When to Heaven I'll be going.

And, Lord you can come and take me home anytime.

"And do not be conformed to this world, but be transformed by the renewing of your mind, that you may prove what is that good and acceptable and perfect will of God."
– Romans 12:2 (NKJV)

Molded Man

Satan's working in this world

And doing all he can

In trying to turn everyone

Into a "molded man".

Molded and conformed

To the ways of the world.

Not knowing of, nor caring for,

The teachings of God's Word.

The Bible tells us not to be

Conformed to worldly ways.

Instead we are to be transformed

From the world, it says.

But, Satan tries to mold us

Into overlooking sin.

Being "Godly" is old fashioned now

For worldliness is "in".

Molded man?

Praise God, that's not what I am.

For Jesus broke the mold and set me free.

Free from sin

For now I am a Christian

And the things of this world don't interest me.

Listen to your radio,

Watch your TV set.

It's plain to see that Satan's

Far from giving up just yet.

The lyrics of the songs they sing,

The stories in the shows,

Are subtle ways that Satan has

Of working with his mold.

Molded man?

Praise God, that's not what I am.

For Jesus broke the mold and set me free.

Free from sin

For now I am a Christian

And the things of this world don't interest me.

"Rejoice, and be exceeding glad: for great is your reward in heaven." - Matthew 5:12 (NKJV)

One of These Days

One of these days

I'll be with Jesus.

One of these days

I'll shake the hand of my Lord.

And, He'll say, "Welcome home my faithful servant,

Now enter in to your reward."

One of these days

I'll go to Glory.

One of these days

Eternity will begin.

Then we will all meet up there with Jesus

And forever we'll be with Him.

But, 'til that day

I'll live for Jesus

And daily seek to do His will.

Yes, one of these days

We'll meet again up in Heaven.

How do I know?

He said we will.

One of these days

Judgment's coming.

One of these days

This world will be here no more.

So do not strive for earthly possessions,

But seek the Lord, He offers more.

"And all these blessings shall come upon you and overtake you, because you obey the voice of the Lord your God."
- Deuteronomy 28:2 (NKJV)

Let the Blessings Flow

I remember long ago

Then the Lord I didn't know.

He was just someone who I had heard of.

When to the altar I went,

I kneeled and prayed and wept.

Then felt the power of His great love.

All my sins He washed away

As He saved my soul that day.

I felt a feeling I can't explain.

Then as I rose to my feet

And felt that sweet peace

I couldn't help but shout out and say...

Let the blessings flow.

Let them flood my soul.

Every good thing comes from the Lord

So let the blessings flow.

And my life since that day

Has been blessed in many ways,

Although I've had my ups and my downs.

But, through the bad times I've learned

To depend more on Him.

For all things will work out for the good.

And, the joy and the peace

That I felt have not ceased.

In fact, they seem to grow more each day.

And, the closer I walk

With my heavenly Lord,

The more the blessings come my way.

Let the blessings flow.

Let them flood my soul.

Every good thing comes from the Lord

So let the blessings flow.

"You will show me the path of life; in Your presence is fullness of joy; at Your right hand are pleasures forevermore." – Psalms 16:11 (NKJV)

It's Just Me and Jesus

I tried the pleasures that this world had to offer

Searching for happiness.

I had money, I had women,

Fancy cars, and all the rest.

All these things were fine for a while,

But I knew there must be something more.

These worldly pleasures couldn't bring true contentment.

Not the contentment that I found in the Lord.

Now it's just me and Jesus.

It's just me and Jesus.

He's true happiness.

And, if I never had ever found Him,

Oh, the contentment that I would have missed.

The search is over

For in the Lord

I found what I'd been searching for.

Now it's just me and Jesus; it's just me and Jesus.

Who could ask for more?

He's my Lord and He's my Savior.

He's my God and He's my King.

He's my strength and He's my courage.

He's my all, my everything.

He is love and the hope for tomorrow.

He's the calm for life's raging storm.

As we walk this road together,

He's my guide to lead me home.

Now it's just me and Jesus.

It's just me and Jesus.

He's true happiness.

And, if I never had ever found Him,

Oh, the contentment that I would have missed.

The search is over

For in the Lord

I found what I'd been searching for.

Now it's just me and Jesus; it's just me and Jesus.

Who could ask for more?

"Pray without ceasing." - 1 Thessalonians 5:17 (KJV)

My Prayer

Lord, never let me say an unkind word

Or perform an unkind deed.

Never let me turn away a friend,

Especially one who is in need.

Never let me criticize.

Never let me be one who condemns.

In all there is about me, Lord,

Let me be worthy of my friends.

Lord, let me have love and show forgiveness

Unto those who do me wrong.

When faced with trials or temptations,

Let my faith in you be strong.

Let me be a witness, Lord.

Never let me lead someone astray.

May everything about me, Lord,

Be an example of your way.

And, when the world has got me down,

Teach me, Lord, to always look above.

And, may my faith and works somehow

Make me worthy of your love.

"For by grace are ye saved through faith; and that not of yourselves: it is the gift of God: Not of works, lest any man should boast." - Ephesians 2:8-9 (KJV)

You Can't Buy Your Way Into Heaven

Now, you can't buy your way into Heaven.

So, let's stop all this preaching on monetary giving.

They preach give God this and give God that

And then they pass around the hat,

But you can't buy your way into Heaven.

Well, I give my offering

And I give God's tithe.

I give back to God as He has supplied.

I go to church nearly every week,

But it seems too often when the preacher speaks

He's talking of money and of what the church owes.

It seems he's more concerned with the wallets than the souls.

But, you can't buy your way into Heaven.

So, let's stop all this preaching on monetary giving.

They preach give God this and give God that

And then they pass around the hat,

But you can't buy your way into Heaven.

There are folks I know

And I think highly of.

They believe in God and in Heaven above.

But, when Sunday comes they stay at home

Because it seems each time that to church they've gone

The preacher's preached church budget again.

They've never once heard him preach salvation's plan.

No, you can't buy your way into Heaven.

So, let's stop all this preaching on monetary giving.

They preach give God this and give God that

And then they pass around the hat,

But you can't buy your way into Heaven.

No, you can't buy your way into Heaven.

"Trust in the Lord with all thine heart; and lean not unto thine own understanding. In all thy ways acknowledge him, and he shall direct thy paths." - Proverbs 3:5-6 (KJV)

Solutions From You

Dear Lord, this world has its problems.

And Lord, I have my problems, too.

So why can't this world learn to do as You have taught me

And seek the solutions from You?

Dear Lord, You are our Creator.

So, who would know better than You

All the troubles and trials that we may encounter

And the way to deal with them, too?

Yes Lord, this world has its problems.

And Lord, I have my problems, too.

I pray that this world will soon do as You have taught me

And seek the solutions from You.

"Behold, I stand at the door and knock. If anyone hears My voice and opens the door, I will come in to him and dine with him, and he with Me." - Revelations 3:20 (NKJV)

He's Standing at Your Heart

Listen, for the Savior

Is speaking now to you,

"I'll give you salvation

If you but ask me to.

I will give you peace and love

And joy forevermore.

I'm standing at your heart now.

Won't you open up the door?"

"I want your soul that I might save it.

If you but ask, I'll cleanse it from all sin.

I want your mind that I might fill it with my word.

I want your heart that I might dwell therein."

Friend, now won't you heed His call?

He's wanting for you to.

Do you want salvation?

He offers it to you.

Have you longed for peace and joy?

It's yours forevermore.

He's standing at your heart now.

Just open up the door.

He wants your soul that He might save it.

If you but ask, He'll cleanse it from all sin.

He wants your mind that He might fill it with His word.

He wants your heart that He might dwell therein.

"Rejoice, and be exceeding glad: for great is your reward in heaven." – Matthew 5:12a (KJV)

I Have Heaven to Live For

There've been many times when I've felt like dying.

When things just weren't going right for me.

But, at times like these when discouraged

The Lord steps in to remind me…

That I have Heaven to live for

And my Lord up above.

I have Heaven to strive for

When the going gets rough here below.

So my friend, when you're tired of trying.

When nothing seems to matter anymore.

Just remember we have a Lord that still loves us

And a Heaven above for our reward.

Yes, we have Heaven to live for

And our Lord up above.

We have Heaven to strive for

When the going gets rough here below.

"...He asked His disciples, saying, 'Who do men say that I, the Son of Man, am?' So they said, 'Some say John the Baptist, some Elijah, and others Jeremiah or one of the prophets.' He said to them, 'But who do you say that I am?' Simon Peter answered and said, 'You are the Christ, the Son of the living God.'" - Matthew 16:13-16 (NKJV)

Who Do You Say I Am

We can strive so hard for the pleasures of life

They can come to mean so much.

But, are these things the world offers you

Worth more than Jesus' love?

What good would it do if you gained all the world,

But lost your soul to sin?

What reply could you give when it came judgment day

And Jesus asked, "Who do you say I am?"

"Who do you say I am?

Am I merely a myth

Or alive and real today?

Am I Savior and friend?

Am I Lord of your life

Or just someone who you've turned away?"

There will come a day when you'll hear a voice

Asking you what was asked long ago,

"Who do you say I am?" – what's your answer to be?

Can you answer, "My Jesus, You are Lord!"?

"Who do you say I am?

Am I merely a myth

Or alive and real today?

Am I Savior and friend?

Am I Lord of your life

Or just someone who you've turned away?"

Is He someone who you've turned away?

"Fear not; for I am with you. Be not dismayed; for I am your God. I will strengthen you; yea, I will help you; yea, I will uphold you with the right hand of My righteousness."
- Isaiah 41:10 (KJV)

I Would Have Never Made It On My Own

I never know from day to day what life has in store,

But there is someone who knows long before I know.

And, He's been there in the good times and through sorrows, too.

He will remedy the hurt if I ask Him to.

He's been there every time I've needed Him.

And, He's known just what it takes for each situation.

I don't know where I'd be if it hadn't been for Jesus,

But I do know I would have never made it on my own.

The loss of a loved one is hard to bear

When you realize you'll never more have them near.

But, He was there with His love to show to me

That death is not a loss, but a victory.

He's been there every time I've needed Him.

And, He's known just what it takes for each situation.

I don't know where I'd be if it hadn't been for Jesus,

But I do know I would have never made it on my own.

The breakup of a family is a tragic thing.

Regardless of the reason, oh, the heartache it brings.

But, He was there when I thought I'd never make it through

To give strength and to encourage so I could start anew.

He's been there every time I've needed Him.

And, He's known just what it takes for each situation.

I don't know where I'd be if it hadn't been for Jesus,

But I do know I would have never made it on my own.

Printed in Germany
by Amazon Distribution
GmbH, Leipzig